Valeri Sepp

TalliNN

The history of an unusual city

FELISTELLA

2011

One could never confuse this city with any other. Throughout history, Tallinn has been conquered by the Russians, the Swedes, the Poles and the Danes, and each in turn has left its own historic footprint on the city's architecture. Today, Tallinn is a blend of the Gothic and Baroque, a mixture of knights' castles and monasteries, Orthodox sanctuaries and medieval buildings, all living together in perfect harmony. Wandering the labyrinth of serpentine, cobbled streets, visitors are transported back to the distant past of legend and folklore. And, as the sunset's purple glow falls on fifteenth century buildings and torches and lanterns begin to flicker across the pavement, the cheerful atmosphere of noisy fairs and markets echoes in the streets, enchanting visitors and surrounding them with the ambiance of ancient times.

Tallinn, with its centuries of history, is a fascinating destination for any visitor. Each house or building has its own story to tell, and yet the majority of them somehow resemble each other, primarily because they were all built in the 15th and 16th centuries, during a dynamic period of construction and economic growth. Today, Tallinn is proud of its historic centre and it has retained far more of its original character than perhaps any other northern European capital. It has been justifiably awarded a place in the UNESCO World Heritage Register. The first mention of the city of Tallinn occurs in the year 1154, when the Arabian geographer, Al-Idrisi, described a city referred to as Quoluwany in his papers "A Diversion for the Man Longing to Travel to Far-Off Places".

Town Hall Square

Old Town has always been the heart of the city of Tallinn. The winding labyrinth of narrow streets and alleys leaves a lasting impression and the city never fails to enchant visitors with its fairy-tale scenes. While it's a well-known fact that "all roads lead to Rome", in the city of Tallinn all roads lead to the Town hall square. Rather remarkably, it was not until fairly recently (in 1923) that the square received its present name. One of the first names it bore was *Markt* (which translates as "market"). The Town Hall Square, reasonably modest in size, is surrounded by a variety of antique buildings, each with a story of its own. In ancient times, a pillory was placed in the centre of the square, where thieves and criminals sentenced to death were beaten before being executed. Still today, one can see a metal collar at-

tached to the building of the Town hall as well as a set of small rings for arms and legs, layered, not with centuries-old rust but possibly with the blood of their unhappy victims. These formed a rather small pillory, a place where people were held for the minor crimes and offences, such as dishonesty in trade, failure to repay debts and fraudulent commercial practices. Nowadays, many festivals and fairs are held here, where skilled artisans and craftsmen exhibit their wares. Christmas was first celebrated in Tallinn in the Town Hall Square in 1441. As was the practice earlier in history, a Christmas tree is set up in the square each December, and a bustling Christmas fair runs throughout the holiday season, offering visitors the chance to hear both medieval and modern music while sipping hot mulled wine.

Town Hall

The first written record of the main building of the square, the Town Hall of Tallinn, dates back to 1322. Over the course of many years, the Town Hall building underwent a continual process of rebuilding and new features constantly appeared. As such, the present look of the Town Hall is the result of substantial reconstruction.

On top of the Town hall, the spire is crowned with a weather vane, affectionately known by the people as "**Old Toomas**" (*Vana Toomas*). The figure visible on the Town Hall today is a replica of the original, which was made in 1530 and now resides in the City Museum. According to legend, a poor widow-fisherwoman once lived in the Fish Port. Her sole source of joy was her son, Toomas. Like any other boy, he worked hard, mastering his skills in archery. Each year, he eagerly waited for the annual archer's contest, held in the month of May in front of the Great Sea Gate, in the Parrot's Garden. A painted, wooden parrot was placed on a high pole, and the one who succeeded in knocking the bird off its pedestal was awarded the Silver Cup of the Great Guild. One day, before the start of the contest, little Toomas appeared in the Parrot's Garden. He had become the best archer among his peers, and, as his fellows began mocking him, he, without thinking, fired an arrow at the wooden parrot. Although his arrow struck home and he knocked the parrot from its place, instead of being awarded

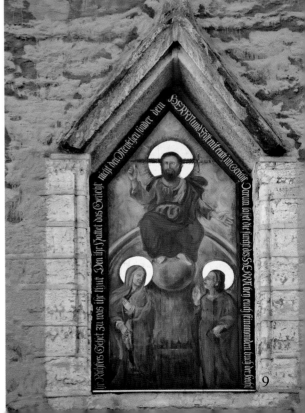

9

⇧ *"Old Toomas"*

the title of "King of the Archers" the boy was reprimanded and was forced to return the parrot to its pole, since the archer's contest had not yet begun. The news of what had happened before the start of the contest spread quickly around the city and Toomas' mother feared the punishment that was sure to be meted out to her child. However, the outcome of the matter was entirely different. The elder of the Great Guild summonsed Toomas and offered him a position in the town watch as an apprentice. This was a delightful prospect for both the mother and her son, for the Guild supplied the watchmen with clothing and food. The years passed and little Toomas grew into a man. He fought in the Livonian Wars and rose to the rank of 'standard-bearer'. By then, he became known as Old Toomas and, since he wore a moustache and was dressed exactly as the warrior figure on the weather vane of the town hall, the citizens nicknamed the weather vane after him – "Old Toomas". The name survived and still lives on today.

In the basement of the Town hall were located various warehouse premises, while

Hall of Magistrates ⇨

the torture chamber, large trade hall, and the state treasury facilities were located on the ground floor. The second floor housed a large hall for the Burghers, in which various receptions took place and feasts were held. Manufactured by the Tallinn grand piano factory, the hall doors are finished in black lacquer and are rather reminiscent of the cover of a grand piano. Also in this space, on the second floor, is the Magistrate's Hall, where the city fathers held their meetings and administrated justice. Only a small number of the Town Hall's antique decorations are displayed within its premises. For example, the town clerks' bench (325 cm in length), made in 1374, is stored in the City Museum. However, the built-in cupboards in the Magistrate's Hall are on display, trimmed with forged, Gothic doors, manufactured at the beginning of the 15th century. Only the sides of the Burgermeisters' first bench remain. On one of the sides is pictured the battle of Samson and the Lion, an allegory of sorts for the eternal fight between good and evil. On the inside of the second bench, a large rose is depicted, symbolizing a silence. There are five large ceiling lamps in the Hall of Magistrates, a perfect example of 18th century Baroque design. The front elevation of the Town Hall is decorated with offsets in the form of dragon-heads, manufactured in 1627. It was a widely held belief in ancient times that such figures would ward off evil spirits.

Hall of the Burghers ⇨

The Town Hall Pharmacy

The first mention of the Town Hall Pharmacy was recorded on April 8, 1422. The medieval pharmacy looked more like a small shop than a modern chemist's shop. One could buy not only medicines in the chemist's shop, but also playing cards, smoking pipes, ink colours, tobacco and even gunpowder.

Prior to the year 1580, there was much coming and going among pharmacists. One might rent a chemist's shop from a magistrate, and within short order end up enlisted as an officer. In the spring of 1580, however, a qualified pharmaceutical chemist, a certain Johann Burchart Belavary de Sykava, arrived from Hungary. From that time on, the history of the pharmacy was closely intertwined with the Burchart family. Thus, in the year 1725, Peter I sought medical advice from Burchart the Fifth, who was widely reputed to have a broad knowledge in the field of the medical sciences. During those ancient times, chemist's shops were not limited to selling medication and drugs. The pharmacy was just as much a gathering place for the town's people. Just as the Town Hall was a place for making important decisions , so too, was the chemist's shop a place for discussion of important political and trade matters.

Discussions usually took place over a glass of claret, which was traditionally flavoured with spices and complimented with so-called "morseli" biscuits, made in the pharmacy. The claret of the Town Hall Pharmacy was prepared according to a special recipe, which has remained unchanged through the years. Even today, one can buy claret in the chemist's shop as a souvenir, prepared in accordance with the special hundred-year-old recipe.

Upper and Lower Town

Tallinn is composed of two different cities: Toompea ("**Upper Town**" or "Vyshgorod" as it is sometimes called) and "**Lower Town**". The Lower Town was built during the 14th to 16th centuries and was inhabited by craftsmen and free citizens. The Upper Town was erected during the 13th and 14th centuries. Toompea was the place of residence of knights, gentry and clergy. Each of the cities had their own laws. What was allowed for the citizens of Toompea was forbidden for the merchants of the Lower Town and vice versa. Relations between the two cities were strained for many years and serious conflicts occurred in matters of trade, judicial power, territorial ownership rights and so on. There was a Town Wall, and gates separating the cities were locked at night. The city of Toompea was the seat of power for the majority of North Estonia, though the Lower Town was authorized to retain its own local administrative powers. The power to rule the Lower Town was granted to the Tallinn magistrate, comprised of 24 magistrates and town clerks.

⇧ *"Short Leg" street*

Pikk yalg and Lühike yalg streets

Lühike yalg and Pikk yalg streets connect the Lower Town with the Upper Town. The name of the latter is well supported by a fanciful metal drain in the form of a huge boot, with slots in the sole allowing for water drainage. The Estonian *Pikk jalg* translates as "**Long Leg**", and *Lühike jalg* as "**Short Leg**". For this reason, Tallinn is jokingly referred to as the "lame" town. From 1454 to 1455, a wall was erected along Long Leg Street (*Pikk yalg*). Both of the towers above the gates of Pikk yalg and Lühike yalg streets have survived. Moreover, above the Lühike yalg tower you can still see a heavy, oak door, trimmed with an abundance of forged metal fittings and broad heads, which look up towards Upper Town and a sturdy antique lock on the opposite side of the door, facing Lower Town. During the times when the tower was equipped with two such doors, these, as well as a hammered metal grill, were locked for the night hours and all communication between the Upper and Lower Towns ceased until dawn.

"Long Leg" street ⇨

Toompea Castle and Tall Hermann

In the summer of 1219, the Danes had conquered the ancient settlement of the Ests and had built a fortress on the southeast side of **Toompea** Hill. Soon after the Danes conquest, the Hill was taken over by the Knights of the Brothers of the Sword. By order of the Master, the Danes' fortress was reconstructed as a castle of Roman design, that is, as a rectangle oriented to the points of the compass.

As a result, Upper Town became completely separated from Lower Town. While power in Lower Town had long been concentrated in the hands of the merchant magistrate, on Toompea, there had been an almost constant shifting of power. After the time of the Knights of the Brothers of the Sword, the Toompea castle was again captured by the Danes and subsequently, for more than two centuries, came under the rule of the Livonian Order. The Poles conquered the castle in 1561. They had established their rule for only two months, when power on Toompea was handed over to Sweden. Finally, in the year 1710, military forces of Peter I entered Revel and Estonia became a part of the Russian State.

Each of the castle's rulers made alterations according to their own needs. In the southwestern corner of the castle, a strong, high tower was erected, called **Tall Hermann** (46.6 metres). The lower level was originally designed as warehouse premises. However, throughout history, it was always used as a prison. In the gloomy underground floor,

devoid of windows and doors, medieval prisoners and those who had participated in rebellions and revolutions whiled away their days.

In the course of the revolution, in 1922, the castle building was burnt to the ground. In its place, the building of the State Council of the Estonian Republic was erected. The south wing of the Palace was built in 1935. The Government of Estonia (*Riigikogu*) is housed in the Palace of Toompea to this day. Today, the blue-black-and-white Estonian flag is raised daily at sunrise, over Tall Hermann, to the strains of the national anthem and is lowered at sunset.

Alexander Nevsky Cathedral

Facing the Parliament building is the magnificent Russian Orthodox Alexander Nevsky Cathedral. The cathedral was built to a design conceived by Russian architect Mikhail Preobrazhenskiy, in 1900. Its construction was dedicated to the Prince of the city of Novgorod, Alexander Nevsky. Many times, the cathedral was threatened with destruction. Fortunately, however, this has never come to pass. The five-domed cathedral with three altars, for the accommodation of 1500 people, was designed according to the Moscow cathedrals of the 17th century. The façades of the cathedral were decorated with mosaics designed by the Academy

member A.N.Frolov. The most powerful ensemble of church bells in the city resounds from the cathedral. Before the commencement of services, the sounds of the cathedral bells spread over the city. All 11 bells of the cathedral were moulded in Saint Petersburg at the bell factory of Vasiliy Orlov. The biggest bell weighs almost 16 tons. The cathedral's interior is richly decorated with mosaics and icons. The icons were created in the workshop of the artist A.N. Novoskoltsev. Saint Petersburg master Steinke produced stained glass to be set in the altar windows according to his sketches. Alexander Nevsky Cathedral is subordinate to the Patriarch of Moscow and all Russia. It has long been a place of service of the Patriarch Aleksiy II.

Linda

In accordance with the legend of the national epic *"Kalevipoeg"*, after the death of her beloved husband Kalev, Linda began gathering stones around his tomb. With these, she planned to erect a monument to him, to ensure that his descendants would forever remember him. One day, while carrying one of these stones, Linda stumbled and the heavy stone dropped from her shoulder. Unable to lift the heavy stone again, the widow sat down on it and began to cry bitterly. In this way, lake Ülemiste was formed and Toompea hill remained the place of Kalev's repose. In 1920, on *Lindamägi* (Little Linda's Hill) in the Swedish stronghold, a bronze replica of the statue of "Linda" was set up. The original was created in 1880 by the Estonian sculptor and Academy member, A. Weitzenberg.

Dome Church

Dome Church is a monument of art, hand made by craftsmen and consecrated as St. Mary's Cathedral in 1240. The first written record of it goes back to the year 1233. Originally, the church was constructed of wood, and only after some time did the black friars rebuild it, using limestone. Fires, wars and pillaging have left their mark upon the decoration of the cathedral, which, in any event, was never particularly ornate or luxurious. The interior is austere and practical, distinctly free of any excess décor. Sculptures of Jesus Christ, St. Mary and John the Baptist surround the 17th century baroque, carved altar of the Dome Church. The most precious items in the church are tombstones, dating from the 13th to 18th centuries, as well as multiple coats of arms and epitaphs of the 17th to 20th centuries. More than 100 coats of arms hang in the Dome cathedral. These emblems indicated the nobility and rank of a family, its status, and some even contain the family name. On the south wall of the altar area, one can see the memorial headstone of the Swedish military commander, Pontus de la Gardi and his wife Princess Sofia Gullenhelm. There is a depiction of the commander himself on the upper plate, in which he wears knight's armour. His wife is depicted beside him, in a magnificent dress carved in stone. On the sides, there is an anaglyph with a view of Narva and the River Narova. This is the

most ancient depiction of the city of Narva, still preserved in our day.

There is one other remarkable tombstone, albeit of a less illustrious historical figure, placed directly in front of the entrance. Here was buried a certain Otto Johan Tuve, well known as a local ladies' man and wine bibber. Shortly before his death, when it became apparent that it would soon be his turn to leave this world, he asked to be buried near the entrance of the Dome cathedral. This was supposedly so that all those who entered would while praying and bowing, at the same time redeem him from his numerous sins. However, according to some accounts, he requested this particular placement so as to be able to cast glances under passing women's skirts even after death.

3

Kiek in de Kök

The tower first figured in history in 1475. Since the Town Wall could not possibly provide sufficient protection, a decision was made to build a defensive tower to protect the western area of the city. When finished, this tower became the strongest in the entire fortification system of Revel. Originally, Kiek in de Kök was built in the shape of a horse-shoe, but later it was reconstructed and took on a circular form. The tower's name was first mentioned in 1577, as "Kyck in de Kaeken". It was subsequently renamed on numerous occasions and today we know it as "*Kiek in de Kök*". Guards keeping watch on the tower observed that, even in the most adverse weather conditions, from the upper storeys of the tower it was possible to look down through the chimneys into the dwellings below and discover what Revel's house-wives might be preparing for dinner. This interesting fact explains the etymology of the tower's curious name: a Lower-Saxon phrase that literally translates as "*Take a look in the kitchen*". In the 18th century, the tower lost its defence function and was used, among other things, as a gunpowder storehouse and as apartment accommodations. In recent years, the tower has housed a museum, with exhibits describing the history of the fortification system of the city of Tallinn.

⇦ *Maiden Tower*   ⇧ *"Wheel Well"*

Maiden Tower

Beside the Kiek in de Kök is another equally interesting tower, the **Maiden Tower** (*Neitsitorn*), erected in the second part of the 14th century. In the Medieval ages, the tower served as a prison for maidens of loose morals. According to another version of history, young women were held here, who would not agree to walk the aisle with the bridegroom of their parents' choosing. Throughout history, the Maiden Tower has repeatedly suffered substantial damage. In each case it was restored, but with major alterations. According to popular belief, the tower was also haunted by ghosts.

"Wheel Well"

On *Rataskaevu* Street ("Wheel Well" street) is the world's only "monument to a wheel well". Long ago, there actually was a functioning well at this location, known as the "**Wheel Well**". It was first mentioned in 1375 and eventually gave the street its present-day name. However, the well's water contained an enormous amount of limestone and was thus quite inappropriate for drinking purposes. Also referred to as the "Cat's Well", it remained in use until the mid 19th century, when it was closed.

St. Nicholas' Church

German merchants, who moved to the city of Tallinn from Gotland Island, founded **St. Nicholas' Church** (*Niguliste kirik*). The church acquired its original form in the 13th century and actually looked more like a fortress. The church was used as a warehouse for goods and was a place for establishing trade deals. Throughout the medieval centuries, the church was richly decorated with numerous objects of art made in Lübeck, the capital of the Hanseatic League to which the city of Tallinn belonged. Historically, this was a Catholic church. However, during the period of the Reformation, it became a Lutheran church. St. Nicholas' Church is the only church in Lower Town fortunate enough to have survived the devastations of the Reformation period of 1523. At one point, all of the locks on the church doors were encased in lead and the irate crowds simply could not force their way inside. Unfortunately, the church was badly damaged in a later bombing raid by the Soviet Air Force and the building was left half destroyed. Many of the works of art were destroyed, though the most valuable of them were saved. Among the magnificent decorative figures in the church that survived was the main altar (width, when opened, 632 cm). Crafted in late Gothic style, it was made in Lübeck by the German artist, Germen Rode. The painted panels of the altar depict the history of St. Nicholas and St. Victor's lives. After the building was reconstructed and its interior renovated, a museum and a concert hall were established in its premises. Priceless exhibits of medieval age art are also on display in the church.

The fragments of Bernt Notke's canvas

"**Dance of a Death**" (end of the 15ᵗʰ century) are of great historical value. At the start of the Reformation, the theme of equality among noblemen and commoners was widely propagated. This theme of equality among the representatives of the 24 estates existing at the time is also apparent in Notke's work. Death, in the form of a skeleton, is depicted alongside each character in the painting. The 30 meter long canvas, preserved in Lübeck, displays all 48 figures, whereas the Tallinn fragment comprises only 13 of those. However, this rare canvas is still of great value, since, of all other renditions of this work in the world, almost none have managed to survive. Additionally, a unique collection of silver items previously owned by the church, the guilds and Brotherhood of Black Heads is kept in the St. Nicholas' Church.

Bernt Notke. "Dance of a Death" ⇩

The Holy Spirit Church

The Holy Spirit Church (*Püha-vaimu kirik*), situated near the Town Hall, is the smallest and oldest place of worship in Lower Town. It was first mentioned in 1316 and originally, was a refuge for the poor. The church's physical orientation was rather at odds with Christian traditions of the times. Usually, the churches were to be oriented with their axes pointing east west. The Holy Spirit Church was erected, facing an entirely different direction: in a south-west to north-east orientation.

The church was reconstructed and expanded many times and in the 17th century an octagonal spire was added. On the wall next to the entrance, Tallinn's oldest clock has been marking time for the past four centuries. It is the only street clock in the city – a most beautiful work of art, decorated with carvings and figures of the evangelists created by Christian Akkerman. One of the church's most valuable works of art is the altar, created in the year of 1483 by Lübeck master, Bernt Notke. In the centre of

the altar is the sculptured composition, "The Descent of the Holy Spirit", and the side panels are decorated with paintings and sculptures of the saints. In the 17th century, pictorial decoration of the choir stalls was added, which included 57 pictures from the Biblical plot "**Biblia Pauperum**" (The Paupers' Bible). The Holy Spirit Church occupies a special place in the history of Estonia. The first sermons ever to be conducted in the Estonian language were delivered here, and the famous Estonian chronicler, Baltazar Russov, conducted worship services in the church. A catechism, published in 1535 by the church's pastor Johann Koell, is thought to be the first book published in the Estonian language.

House of the Brotherhood of Black Heads

The main social organization of Revel was the Great Guild. Its members were required to comply with specific membership conditions, including the clause of the Guild dictating that its members be married. Bachelor merchants, in turn, had united to establish their own organization called the Brotherhood of Black Heads. This association, like all of the guilds, originally was comprised of a Christian community, gathering around one of the churches and supporting it. After the Reformation, these close connections with the churches weakened and the guilds turned into associations of people of high society, each guild organized according to the main occupation of its members. The founding date of the Brotherhood of Black Heads is considered to be 1399. In accordance with the Charter of the Brotherhood, the "Black Heads" were obliged to defend their people, take part in city celebrations, and receive prominent guests. The name of the Brotherhood is connected with the fearless Negro Christian warrior, Saint Maurice, who had become the patron saint of the Brotherhood and whose bust appears on the emblem of the Black Heads. The Brotherhood functioned only within the territory of Estonia and Latvia, and was quite unknown in western Europe during medieval times.

Among the most significant events of the Brotherhood were the mass feasts and dinners, held on the eve of a main holiday.

26

№ 170

43

On these occasions, new members were introduced. The feasts were organized four times a year, the main ones being the Christmas and Easter feasts. These ended with a Mass in St. Catherine's church, and those absent at these events would be punished with a fine. Family events, such as weddings and funerals, also served as occasions for large feasts. The organization survived through various periods of upheaval until the year 1895, when it was liquidated as an estate organization. The Black Heads Club continued to exist thereafter, as a secular organization, until 1940.

One of the most valuable works of art to survive until our day is a 15th century side altar. It was called the "Altar of the Black Heads" and was originally located in the Dominican monastery. After the Reformation, the altar was set in the building of the Brotherhood of Black Heads where it remained untouched for several centuries.

The façade of the building of the Brotherhood of Black Heads figures prominently in the collection of Dutch Renaissance art. The Frieze, between the first two levels, is trimmed with the emblems of the largest Hanseatic trade agencies: Bruges, Novgorod, London and Bergen. Here you can see the images of Christ, the Goddess of Justice and Peace, and depictions of knight's tournaments and contests. Over the windows of the first stage were placed the sculptural portraits of King Sigismund and his wife, Anna of Austria. On the façade one can also see textured masonry work depicting two lions holding the Brotherhood emblem featuring the head of St. Maurice. On both sides of the entrance hang the sole surviving entry shields made of carved stone.

A Green market

Not far from the House of the Brotherhood of Black Heads, at the intersection of Pikk and Olevimyagi streets, is the **Green Market** (*Roheline turg*). The name of the market is not associated with the centuries-old trees growing nearby, as one might expect. Indeed, there are almost no trees growing anywhere in Lower Town and the trees are a unique feature of the area. The etymology of the name 'green market' takes us far back into history, when the vegetables and "greens" market was located here. Tallinn's oldest tree, surrounded by a low fence, stands nearby, as well as a parking area filled with hundreds of cars. In the corner of the Green Market is a small Orthodox chapel, built in 1909.

Three sisters

Like all women, the "Three Sisters" refuse to reveal the year of their birth. The "Three Sisters" are three merchant houses, literally merged into one another. The history of the three sisters can be traced back to at least 1362. For six and a half centuries, the owners of these houses were the Guilds elders, members of the city magistrate and even town mayors. Each new owner reconstructed the building to suit his own taste and needs. At various stages of history, the buildings have also housed both communal living quarters and tourist administration offices. Eventually, one particular owner opened a five-star hotel here, which has become very popular among high standing officials of state. The Queen of England and the Emperor of Japan have stayed here, and one of the first guests of the hotel was Lennart Meri (former president of Estonia) who arrived for a private visit.

St. Olav's Church

When approaching Old Town, one cannot fail to notice the spire of **St. Olav's Church** (*Oleviste Kirik*, in Estonian). It embodies the mighty power of the city and, standing on higher ground as it does, even in medieval times defined the silhouette of the city. The spire is visible at a distance and often served as a point of reference for seamen. At one stage in history, St. Olav's Church was the highest structure in the world, thanks to its lofty spire. It now reaches to a height of 124 metres, and the church has become a defining symbol of the city of Tallinn. However, such an impressive height bears with it a serious danger. The church has been struck by a

lightning eight times in its history and on three of those occasions ended up engulfed in flames. No one knows the exact date of the first construction of the church. Nevertheless, history makes mention of a trading courtyard used by Scandinavian merchants on the spot, and the church has been standing in this location since at least the 12th century. The first official record of the church bears the date of 1267. In the 15th century, the church was almost completely reconstructed. New choir stalls were created and the longitudinal section of the building was turned into a basilica with four-sided columns. The arches of the central area formed a stellate, and the side arches, a cross. From 1513 to 1523, St. Mary's Chapel was joined to the structure, also known as the "Bremen Chapel". After the fire of June 16, 1820, the church was repaired and acquired the familiar look that we see today. This reconstruction marked the start of neo-Gothic style in the construction of Estonian churches. According to the design of artist Friedrich Ludwig von Maidell, the altar and pulpit, church pews, carved window frames and doors were created. On the outside eastern wall of the chapel a cenotaph (honorary monument) was set in place, dedicated to the Prior of the parish, Hans Pavels. Eight bas-reliefs depict the last days of Jesus Christ's life. In the lower row, from left to right, are: "The entrance of our Lord into Jerusalem", "The Lord's Supper", "Christ in the Garden of Gethsemane", "Jesus Arrested". The upper row depicts, from left to right: "Jesus Interrogated by the High Priest Caiaphas", followed by other scenes mentioned in the Gospels: "And the soldiers wove a crown of thorns, and put it on his head, and they struck him with their hands", "Jesus before Pilate" and the last bas-relief "Jesus Arrested". Today, the church is the largest church building in Estonia and is owned by the Evangelical Christian Baptists, the third-largest Christian religion in the republic.

Viru Gates

The Viru Gates were built in the 14th century and have only partly survived. They are situated in the eastern part of the Town Wall that surrounds Tallinn's Old Town. These two towers wrapped in green are "gates in time". They lead from a modern city full of skyscrapers to the historic and most fascinating part of Tallinn. Viru Street, with its numerous shops, cafes and restaurants covers the approximately 200 meters leading up to the Viru Gates.

St. Catherine's Passage

St. Catherine's Passage (*Katariina Käik*) is considered to be one of the most romantic streets of Tallinn's Old Town. It connects *Vene* (Russian) and *Müürivahe* (inter-wall) streets and has become a well-known spot for browsing workshops and craftsmen's shops, and watching artisans at work. Here, visitors will find potters, leatherworkers, glass blowers, weavers, all busy at work just as they would have been long ago, in medieval times.

Town Fortifications and Fat Margaret

The most impressive architectural achievement of the medieval master masons was the Town Wall. The wall took almost 300 years to build, and formed a powerful system of fortifications for the city. In 1355, a magistrate produced the first list of towers of the Town Wall, which indicates that at that time, there were 11 towers. During the second half of the 14th century and the early 15th century, many new towers appeared, finally amounting to a grand total of 46. From this system of

fortifications, 26 towers have survived, as well as 1,850 meters of the wall.

Because of the fortress wall, Tallinn took on the same rounded shape from the south and from the east. Town Hall Square was no longer on the edge of the city, but rather, ended up at its centre, where the most important streets and roads leading to the city came together. *Müürivahe* (inter-wall) Street appeared near the new Town Wall and linked the streets leading away from the Town Hall. For centuries it remained the main road for supplying the City Wall and defensive towers.

At the beginning of the 16th century, the next stage of intensive construction of Town Wall began. It was at this time that the Town Wall of Tallinn acquired the final shape that we see today. This further construction was necessitated by the development of firearms and the introduction of mines and cannon fire, which could easily destroy the fortress walls. In addition to strengthening the Town Wall, construction was begun on several new towers, which were high and thick-walled. Towers situated directly within the city walls were not sufficient, and thus, construction of the outer gates – Viru Gates and Great Sea Gate – began. Despite the great effort put into building up the fortifications, it was not easy to keep up with the rapid

developments in firearms. The lower part of the Town Wall was poorly secured, as in many of the towers it was impossible to fire shells from the lower floors.

In 1510, construction began on the new, large "**Fat Margaret's Tower**" in front of the Great Sea Gate. This was an artillery tower, which would defend against attack from the sea. The walls of the tower were built to a thickness of 5 metres, the tower itself, 24 metres in diameter, with portals for guns now located on the first floor. With only four floors, Fat Margaret's Tower was very well suited to horizontal defence. The tower was rebuilt several times, and was used as an armoury and served as a prison for 12 years until it was gutted by fire. Today, the tower houses the Estonian Maritime Museum, with its collection of rare artefacts: antique diving and fishing equipment and various objects retrieved from the seabed, among other things. At the top of Fat Margaret's Tower is a viewing platform, providing an excellent view of the sea.

St. Brigitta's Convent

Less than six kilometres east of Old Town are the ruins of medieval St. Brigitta's Convent. At one point, the monastery was the largest monastic structure in Livonia. Three wealthy Tallinn merchants began construction of the convent in 1407 and then decided to make their homes there. Both monks and nuns resided in the monastery. Today, the most impressive part of the entire complex that remains is the western face and a four-sided wall with four openings. The Monastery lasted only 170 years and was destroyed in the years between 1575 and 1577. For the centuries, the ruins were used as a quarry, and the yard in front of the church served as a cemetery. Limestone gravestone crosses date from two centuries ago.

Today, the ruins of the monastery have become a unique attraction and wonderful place for recreation. Open-air concerts are often held here, as well as the Festival of Brigitta. This is a family celebration, accompanied by a craft fair,

folk music and dancing. In 2001, next to the ruins of the ancient monastery, a new limestone monastery building was built, which has become home to the nuns of the Order of St. Brigitta.

Pirita Monastery has given its name to the whole area and today it is one of the most prestigious residential areas in the city. Pirita enjoys wonderful views of the sea and the spires of Old Town and skyscrapers of the modern downtown area are visible in the distance.

Kadriorg

Less than two kilometres from the centre of Tallinn are **Kadriorg** Park and Palace. Construction of the palace began on July 22, 1718 by order of the Russian Emperor, Peter I, with the direct participation of the latter. The king himself laid down three bricks in the wall of the future palace (in the northeast corner of the building). They are still visible, due to the tradition of leaving them un-plastered. The palace was built

as a summer residence for the royal family and was named after the tsar's wife, Catherine I (Kadriorg means "Valley of Catherine" in Estonian). The Park was designed as a promenade for residents and visitors and consists of three parts. In the upper garden are flower-beds and fountains. The lower garden is located directly in front of the palace. Near the lower garden is the picturesque Swan Pond. Unfortunately, Peter I did not live to see the completion of the palace and after the death of the monarch, the palace was only used on rare occasions. Almost all of the Russian emperors stayed here during visits to Tallinn. In 1919, after the overthrow of the tsarist regime, a museum was established in the palace. In 1991 a long period of restoration and repair began and on July 22, 2000, Kadriorg Art Museum opened within the palace, with exhibitions comprising more than 900 paintings of Russian and European pictorial art.

Rusalka (Mermaid)

On the 7th of September 1893, one of the greatest disasters in Baltic maritime history took place. During a violent storm, the Russian battleship "Rusalka (Mermaid)" sank, en route from Revel to Helsingfors. In memory of the 177 members of the crew that perished, the famous Estonian sculptor Amandus Adamson created a monument called "Mermaid". The granite base of the monument is made in the form of a battleship, navigating the waves in a storm. From the deck of the ship a high granite rock rises, with an angel standing at the top. The angel looks out to sea and a golden cross is raised up high in hand, blessing the ships and protecting them from the storm.

Song Festival Grounds

The tradition of Estonian song festivals originated from the first song festival, which took place in June 1869, in the city of Tartu. Song festivals became one of the most important cultural events in

Estonia, and were conducted by **Gustav Ernesaks** (Estonian composer and choral conductor). A monument in his memory stands in the Song Festival Grounds. According to tradition, the song festival is held every five years at the Song Festival Grounds. A huge, open-air concert hall was built in 1960, and can accommodate up to 30,000 singers. Nearby stands a lighthouse. At its top is a bowl in which a fire is lit, during the song festival. In summer, international stars are invited to give their concerts. *The Õlle* (beer) *summer* festival and Pancake Week are held here as well.

Open air museum

The open-air museum is a park-museum located in **Rocca al Mare** (Italian for "a rock by the sea"). The Ethnographic Museum was founded in 1957, and portrays the historic daily life of Estonian peasants of the 18th and 19th centuries. More than 70 buildings have been brought in from around the country and displayed in 12 different estates, consisting of residential and commercial buildings. There are buildings for fishing nets, a smithy, windmills and water mills, a small wooden church, and even a small tavern among them. The interiors of the houses are preserved in their original form. In total, the museum has a collection in excess of 46,000 exhibits. There is a striking abundance of fences in the yards and along the streets. This may be explained by the practice of letting cattle graze freely, typical for that time. The park-museum's collection continues to grow and during the holiday periods, festivities with songs and dances are organized on the grounds.

Tallinn. The history of an unusual city.
Text: Valeri Sepp
Translation: Olga Kotieva
Proofreading: Richard Maxwell, David Maxwell
Photos: Valeri Sepp, Ernest Bondarenko
Design and make-up: Maria Sepp
Publishing house: © Felistella OÜ 2011

Printed in Estonia

ISBN 978-9949-21-744-1
e-mail: info@felistella.eu
www.felistella.eu